# Eleven Po
## about Football

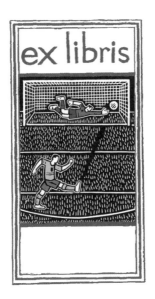

Candlestick Press

Published by:
Candlestick Press,
Diversity House, 72 Nottingham Road, Arnold, Nottingham UK NG5 6LF
www.candlestickpress.co.uk

Design and typesetting by Diversity Creative Marketing Solutions Ltd.,
www.diversity.agency

Printed by Ratcliff & Roper Print Group, Nottinghamshire, UK

Selection and Introduction © Conor O'Callaghan, 2018

Cover illustration © Hugh Ribbans, 2018
www.hughribbans.com

Candlestick Press monogram © Barbara Shaw, 2008

ISBN 978 1 907598 58 6

**Acknowledgements:**

The poems in this pamphlet are reprinted from the following books, all by
permission of the publishers listed unless stated otherwise. Every effort has
been made to trace the copyright holders of the poems published in this book.
The editor and publisher apologise if any material has been included without
permission or without the appropriate acknowledgement, and would be glad to be
told of anyone who has not been consulted. Thanks are due to all the copyright
holders cited below for their kind permission:

Simon Armitage, *The Dead Sea Poems* (Faber & Faber, 1995) by kind permission
of the author and publisher

Tiffany Atkinson, *Catulla et al* (Bloodaxe Books, 2011) www.bloodaxebooks.com

Claire Crowther, *The Clockwork Gift* (Shearsman Books, 2009)

Elaine Feeney, *The Radio was Gospel* (Ireland: Salmon Poetry, 2013)

Miriam Gamble, *The Squirrels are Dead* (Bloodaxe Books, 2011)
www.bloodaxebooks.com

Gill Learner, first appeared in *14 Magazine, Issue 10*, and has since been
published in *The Agister's Experiment* (Two Rivers Press, 2011) by kind
permission of the author

Ian McMillan, for the Premier League and The Poetry Society by whom it was
commissioned, © Ian McMillan, by permission of the author

Seamus Heaney, *Seeing Things* (Faber & Faber, 1991)

Sean O'Brien, *Collected Poems* (Picador, 2012) by kind permission of the author

Conor O'Callaghan, poem first published in this anthology

George Szirtes, *New & Collected Poems* (Bloodaxe Books, 2008)
www.bloodaxebooks.com

Sarah Wardle, *Score!* (Bloodaxe Books, 2005) www.bloodaxebooks.com

Where poets are no longer living, their dates are given.

All permissions cleared courtesy of Swift Permissions
(swiftpermissions@gmail.com)

# Contents

# Introduction

The worlds of football and poetry scarcely overlap. Or do they? Football is, if you think about it, always likening itself to poetry. YouTube is awash with footage of goals that plummy vintage commentators describe as 'pure poetry'. The reverse is also true. Way back in 1883, five years before the formation of the first official league, the great Gerard Manley Hopkins wrote thus to Robert Bridges in a moment of metaphorical self-pity:

> "I have long been Fortune's football and am blowing up the bladder of resolution big and buxom for another kick of her foot."

Poetry, as we learned at school, has subject matter and themes. That simply means that poems describe one thing and are also very often about something bigger. Take Seamus Heaney's 'Markings' which opens the selection. It describes playing football as a kid, and playing so long that dark falls and the ball gradually becomes invisible. The poem is also about that extraordinary everyday moment when instinct takes over from what we know and see. It is about, in a word, inspiration.

This collection of footie-themed poems should provide further proof of the commonality between these apparently separate spheres. Sarah Wardle's 'Against Metaphor', for example, is a witty dispelling of those many figurative images that form football's vocabulary. Then there is the gentle eroticism of Tiffany Atkinson's 'Marzipan Blues' and Elaine Feeney's adolescent crush on Ryan Giggs. Several of the poems use football as a point of entry into larger things. Ian McMillan recalls the match played between British and German soldiers on Christmas Day in 1914. For Sean O'Brien, the packed stands in Newcastle raise issues of class. For Miriam Gamble, George Best's way with the ball was an embodiment of his playful, troubled city of birth.

I hope you find something here that will encourage you to look at football with new eyes, and see its rituals and rivalries in a whole new light.

*Conor O'Callaghan*

## Markings (i)

We marked the pitch: four jackets for four goalposts,
That was all. The corners and the squares
Were there like longitude and latitude
Under the bumpy ground, to be
Agreed about or disagreed about
When the time came. And then we picked the teams
And crossed the line our called names drew between us.

Youngsters shouting their heads off in a field
As the light died and they kept on playing
Because by then they were playing in their heads
And the actual kicked ball came to them
Like a dream heaviness, and their own hard
Breathing in the dark and skids on grass
Sounded like effort in another world...
It was quick and constant, a game that never need
Be played out. Some limit had been passed,
There was fleetness, furtherance, untiredness
In time that was extra, unforeseen and free.

*Seamus Heaney  (1939 – 2013)*

## Against Metaphor

Here Pompey means Portsmouth.
There is no Caesar, or Caesarean.
We're singing because we've won 3-1,
but the landslide isn't literal
and we're on firm ground.

This is not a paddock. The players
are neither trophies nor horseflesh.
This green field is not a scientific pun,
a *Secret Garden* or Sandford Park.
Nor is it the exile of Tiberius.

We're Tottenham till we die,
but no one's being buried here today.
This turf is not the Somme.
Santini's gone, but still alive.
Programmes are not manifestos or hymns.

Police who tell opposition stands to sit
aren't prefects, teachers or Nazis,
or Marxists up the corridor at work.
That angry teenager is not led away
yet. A gull is free to circle and to fly.

Our bodies packed in stands are not
battery hens or meat to feed to cannons.
Slow feet shuffle back to the weekend,
not morning lessons. A sign reads
'Spurs' in the community, not 'care'.

The icon on its orb is not a crucifix.
A cockerel isn't crowing three times.
Here character doesn't lead to tragedy
and human heroism is life not art.
We're in White Hart Lane, not heaven,

though in myth heaven is a place like this.
And this thing we're willing away
from the open posts of our goal
is neither a bomb nor a baby,
but sweet FA, only a bloody ball.


*Sarah Wardle*

# Ryan Giggs is a Ride

*– for Jack*

1.

I stuck Ryan Giggs pictures
on my blue walls,
down on the skirting boards,
match stickers
all over my wardrobe
and on my window sill.

I stuck Ryan Giggs letters
in the green post-box
on the corner of
Court Lane and High Street,

like a desperate pyrotechnic lover.

I begged him to love me so
I stuck in the language of Shakespeare.

I should have
turned up at his door
and asked him for a ride.

Or married his brother.

I wasted lots of paper.

Then we lost contact.

I started wearing
black crushed velvet
and smoking pot.

I started biting my nails hard
and chasing boys with
back issues of *X-Men*.


2.


I married a Liverpool fan
I have a son who wants to be a Liverpool player
I have a son who wants to be a tree

And I stick their photos all
over my side of the bed,
and all down the skirting board,
they're all over our old
paraná pine wardrobe
and even frescoes
on the window-sill,

just for when the
transfer market opens –
and I lose one of them.


*Elaine Feeney*

## Street Football

You could hear new tines of glass, let out like children,
stick the wind. Then the Shrove ball flew above

the greensand caves, yells drumming it north past
the Brewery and the Dust Destructor. It landed on

a drunk, shaking a collecting tin. Back from alleys,
yards and windows, up, up until it staggered

toward Turner, Sauberge – where my mended kettle
was ready on Ash Wednesday – the ball bounced off

the diapers of Chitty's brickwork, sprinkled Nanny Puttock
from her fountain – come in, boys, she beckoned – soared

as far as Pump Corner, brushed black suits hung
along Fielders' window. Tall Percy palmed the last

drop of rain. Because my hands had practised taking
Matchpeller's dog when it sprang, my bones were fit to break

to confiscate the ball and – flash – no-one stopped
a grandmother catch, a game finish. Men boiled over

Master Woodger's muffins. Fattened, Taffer Boult,
dressed as Grandma Wolf, stood up on gouty feet.


*Claire Crowther*

## Autumn Begins at St. James's Park, Newcastle

*homage to James Wright*

Under the arc, the Toon Army tsunami,
Under three o'clock's great cry on Gallowgate,
Remember the lost world, politics: cages flying
Up from the pit and disgorging their democrats,
Helmeted, in blackface, by the thousand,
Like the sappers of the Somme.

A seated army of convicts
Will be thundering WOR BALL
At faintheart southern referees all winter.

At freezing dusk the bloodbucket bars are stowed out.
Mortgaged to football, the underclass raises
A glass to the ghost of itself
In a world without women or work.


*Sean O'Brien*

## Tinkerness

*– in memory of George Best*

Something in the way you man that ball
is endemic to this city.
As you spoon it down the field
you are both barbarian and ballet-
girl: as rough and ready as they come, with a zing
that's ever-so-slightly off the mark.
I can almost hear you saying:
'That thing's as hard as a hoor's heart'
to the notion that something might be fragile,
the injunction to take care
as you blaze seamlessly from goal to goal,
and, latterly, disaster to disaster,
taking life one dance-step at a time,
never thinking about the future, each move
an explosion of your love. A love,

perhaps, that also carried, even in its prime,
a fair share of that 'drug-dull fatalism' ascribed to us:
that had taken from the red-brick terraces of east
Belfast more than anyone could fathom
from the flick of your fleet feet. Snow looms
in the grey sky of your maiden city on this cold
November afternoon, and they interrupt the run of the radio
as you have always interrupted plans,
diving in when you were least expected,
a blur of energy kitted out in black and white and red.
You were the fierce alembic of your homeland,
your dream-runs down and around Cregagh Road
going on to render you ambassador, to wide worlds,
of a certain sideways motion: the last perverse twist;
quips tailor-made in this city of oddments.

*Miriam Gamble*

## Marzipan Blues

Later he tries to explain
the turquoise joy, at ten,
of that first Rangers strip;
his birthday-fingers skidding
on the wrapping's brittle ice.

It's occult, such a shock
of cloth – the sweet, sheer blue
enough to make his teeth ache.
Hard to bear the perfect interval
of white trim at the neck: the brisk

heroic V whose yearning geometry
fits *just so*. It's a humbling ratio,
along the lines of football: stadium;
wee boy: the goals of men. But he's
already elsewhere. And of course

he thinks I wouldn't understand:
I'm pointing like a school-marm
everywhere but at myself. Look –
was the blue like this? I say. Or
this? Well, was it? Anything like this?


*Tiffany Atkinson*

## Preston North End

Tottenham Hotspur versus Preston North End.
Finney's last season: my first. And my dad
with me. How surprisingly well we blend

with these others. Then the English had
the advantage, but today we feel
their fury, sadness and pity. There were some bad

years in between, a lot of down-at-heel
meandering. For me though, the deep blue
of Preston was ravishment of a more genteel,

poetic kind. They were thrashed 5-1, it's true,
and Finney was crocked by Mackay. Preston went down,
hardly to rise again. But something got through

about Finney the plumber, Lancashire, the Crown,
and those new days a-coming. The crowd dissolves,
but we are of the crowd, heading into town

under sodium street lights. This year Wolves
will win the title. Then Burnley. I will see
Charlton, Law and George Best. The world revolves

around them and those voices on TV
reading the results. I'm being bedded in –
to what kind of soil remains a mystery,

but I sense it in my marrow like a thin
drift of salt blown off the strand. I am
an Englishman, wanting England to win.

I pass the Tebbitt test. I am Allan Lamb,
Greg Rusedski, Viv Anderson, the boy
from the corner shop, Solskjaer and Jaap Stam.

I feel no sense of distance when the tannoy
plays Jerusalem, Rule Britannia or the National Anthem.
I know King Priam. I have lived in Troy.


*George Szirtes*

# The Game: Christmas Day, 1914

*It is so cold.*
*The lines of this poem are sinking*
*Into the unforgiving mud. No clean sheet.*

Dawn on a perishing day. The weapons freeze
In the hands of a flat back four.
The moon hangs in the air like a ball
Skied by a shivering keeper.
All these boys want to do today
Is shoot, and defend, and attack.

Light on a half-raised wave. The trench-faces
Lifted till you see their breath.
A ball flies in the air like a moon
Kicked through the morning mist.
All these boys want to have today
Is a generous amount of extra time.

No strict formations here, this morning;
No 4-4-2 or 4-5-1
No rules, really. Just a kickabout
With nothing to be won
Except respect. *We all showed pictures,*
*I learned his baby's name.*
Now clear the lines of this poem
And let's get on with the game.

No white penalty spot, this morning,
The players are all *unknown.*
You can see them in the graveyards
In teams of forgotten stone;
The nets are made of tangled wire,
No Man's Land is the pitch,
A flare floodlights the moments
Between the dugouts and the ditch.

A hundred winters ago sky opened
To the sunshine of the sun
Shining on these teams of players
And the sounds of this innocent game.
All these boys want to hear today
Is the final whistle. Let them walk away.

*It has been so cold. The lines*
*Of these poems will be found, written*
*In the unforgotten mud like a team sheet.*
*Remember them. Read them again.*


*Ian McMillan*

## Goalkeeper with a Cigarette

That's him in the green, green cotton jersey,
prince of the clean sheets – some upright insect
boxed between the sticks, the horizontal
and the pitch, stood with something up his sleeve,
armed with a pouch of tobacco and skins
to roll his own, or else a silver tin
containing eight or nine already rolled.
That's him with one behind his ear, between
his lips, or one tucked out of sight and lit –
a stamen cupped in the bud of his fist.
That's him sat down, not like those other clowns,
performing acrobatics on the bar, or press-ups
in the box, or running on the spot,
togged out in turtleneck pyjama-suits
with hands as stunted as a bunch of thumbs,
hands that are bandaged or swaddled with gloves,
laughable, frying-pan, sausage-man gloves.
Not my man, though, that's not what my man does;
a man who stubs his reefers on the post
and kicks his heels in the stud-marks and butts,
lighting the next from the last, in one breath
making the save of the year with his legs,
taking back a deep drag on the goal-line
in the next; on the one hand throwing out
or snaffling the ball from a high corner,
flicking off loose ash with the other. Or
in the freezing cold with both teams snorting
like flogged horses, with captains and coaches
effing and jeffing at backs and forwards,
talking steam, screaming exhausting orders,
that's not breath coming from my bloke, it's smoke.
Not him either goading the terraces,
baring his arse to the visitors' end
and dodging the sharpened ten-pence pieces,
playing up, picking a fight, but that's him
cadging a light from the ambulance men,

loosing off smoke rings, zeros or halos
that drift off, passively, over the goals
into nobody's face, up nobody's nose.
He is what he is, does whatever suits him,
because he has no highfalutin song
to sing, no neat message for the nation
on the theme of genius or dedication;
in his passport, under 'occupation',
no one forced the man to print the word
'custodian', and in *The Faber Book
of Handy Hints* his five-line entry reads:
'You young pretenders, keepers of the nought,
the nish, defenders of the sweet fuck-all,
think bigger than your pockets, profiles, health;
better by half to take a sideways view,
take a tip from me and deface yourselves.'


*Simon Armitage*

# Exile

*For Bruce*

He left behind the red-brick villas, gravel beds
and lakes of sand spread with the river's flood.

In a land of gritstone walls where flat is rare,
an alien among worshippers of different gods,
he drills his children in the canticles of home.
Before they're old enough to understand,
even less attend the ceremonials,
they can recite the sacred calls,
cheer with same-faith bands who pilgrim north.

At play these infant acolytes rehearse the adult rituals
with a model of the talisman, at an altar improvised
from bricks against the fence. Robed in red, they lift
their shining voices in defiant conjurations:
van Persie, Walcott, Fabregas.


*Gill Learner*

# Coda: from the touchline

## An Irishman Coaches the Beautiful Game in the American South

*Time was I was the guru of soccer,*
*a footie svengali in North Carolina.*

I gave the Piedmont Triad the sweeper system.
Touchlines hushed to my nuggets of wisdom.

T-shirts were printed with my every word.
The European Cup was played on our road.

I took Rush and Dalglish to the Mason Dixie.
I was asked to lead grace over Domino's pizza.

I screamed expletives till the sheriff came calling.
'Take it down a notch, Coach, or we got a problem.'

*Time was I was the guru of soccer,*
*a footie svengali in North Carolina.*

I saw Ossie Ardiles in Oriel Park.
'That a fact, Coach? Well bless your heart…'

I drifted to watch the immigrant workers,
the barefoot pot-bellied dribblers and jugglers

in a circle of dust, playing hooky with a ball,
displaced in a place that's all about goals.

I watched them till dark and the troops filed past.
'Night, Coach. Goodnight.' We were left last.

*Time was I was the guru of soccer,*
*a footie svenagli in North Carolina.*

*Conor O'Callaghan*